MOTORCYCLE RACING

The Fast Track

Hillclimb

JIM MEZZANOTTE

GARETH**STEVENS**

GS

PUBLISHING

A Member of the WRC Media Family of Companies

Please visit our web site at: www.garethstevens.com
For a free color catalog describing Gareth Stevens Publishing's
list of high-quality books and multimedia programs, call
1-800-542-2595 (USA) or 1-800-387-3178 (Canada).
Gareth Stevens Publishing's fax: (414) 332-3567.

Library of Congress Cataloging-in-Publication Data

Mezzanotte, Jim.
   Hillclimb / by Jim Mezzanotte.
      p. cm. — (Motorcycle racing: The fast track)
   Includes bibliographical references and index.
   ISBN 0-8368-6422-0 (lib. bdg.)
   ISBN 0-8368-6571-5 (softcover)
   1. Motorcycle racing—Juvenile literature.
   2. Motorcycles, Racing—Juvenile literature. I. Title.
   GV1060.M48   2006
   796.7'5—dc22   2005027214

This edition first published in 2006 by
Gareth Stevens Publishing
A Member of the WRC Media Family of Companies
330 West Olive Street, Suite 100
Milwaukee, WI 53212 USA

Editor: Leifa Butrick
Cover design and layout: Dave Kowalski
Art direction: Tammy West
Picture research: Diane Laska-Swanke

Technical Advisor: Kerry Graeber

Photo credits: Cover, pp. 5, 7, 9, 11, 13, 15, 17, 19, 21 © David L. Patton, Jr.

Printed in the United States of America

1 2 3 4 5 6 7 8 9 10 09 08 07 06

CONTENTS

Cover: A hillclimb is a wild ride to the top!

The World of Hillclimbing

Want to learn about an exciting, unusual sport? Hillclimbing is a kind of motorcycle racing. Riders speed up steep hills. They do not race against each other. Instead, they race against the clock. The quickest ride to the top wins.

This sport is one of the oldest kinds of motorcycle racing. It first began in the early 1900s. Back then, motorcycles had not been around for very long.

Today, people still compete in hillclimbing. Many hillclimbs take place in the United States. Riders use special bikes with powerful engines. They hit jumps and fly through the air. Hillclimbing is full of wild action!

Dirt goes flying as a rider climbs a hill. The person who climbs it the quickest wins.

U.S. Hillclimbs

In the United States, **pros** compete in a hillclimb championship. AMA Pro Racing sets the rules. It is part of the American Motorcyclist Association, or AMA. Riders earn points in each hillclimb. The one who earns the most points is the champ. There are hillclimbs for **amateurs**, too. Riders of all ages compete.

AMA pro hillclimbs take place in the midwest and east. A hill may have rocks, ledges, and jumps. The bikes race over grass, dirt, or sand. Local motorcycle clubs often host the hillclimbs.

Some riders compete in hillclimbs in the west. Western hills are usually longer than eastern ones. They have turns, and they are often harder to climb.

In amateur hillclimbs, even young riders compete. This rider has a smaller bike than the pros, but it is still fast!

Beat the Clock

Riders climb a hill one at a time. Each rider begins a climb, or run, in the starting box. It is an area at the bottom of the hill. A rider waits until the hill is clear. Then, the rider takes off from the starting box.

A clock starts when a rider leaves the starting box. It stops when the rider reaches the top of the hill. Riders make their runs very quickly. They often reach the top in less than ten seconds. Some runs are more than 500 feet (150 meters) long. Others are shorter.

In hillclimb events, a rider makes two or three runs. The rider with the fastest run wins.

A hill is ready for the next rider. It is very steep, but riders climb it quickly.

9

Long and Lean

In hillclimbing, riders use special bikes. These **custom** bikes are built just for hillclimbs. They are strong but light. They do not have equipment for riding on the street.

When riders climb steep hills, their bikes sometimes flip over backwards. Short bikes flip easily, so hillclimbing bikes are very long. They have an extra long swingarm. The swingarm connects the rear wheel to the bike.

These bikes need good **traction** to climb hills. Some riders put chains on the rear tire. Others use a paddle tire. This tire has big ridges that dig into the ground. Hillclimbing bikes have only one small brake. It is on the front wheel. Riders do not use the brakes much!

This bike is perfect for racing up hills. It cannot be used on regular roads.

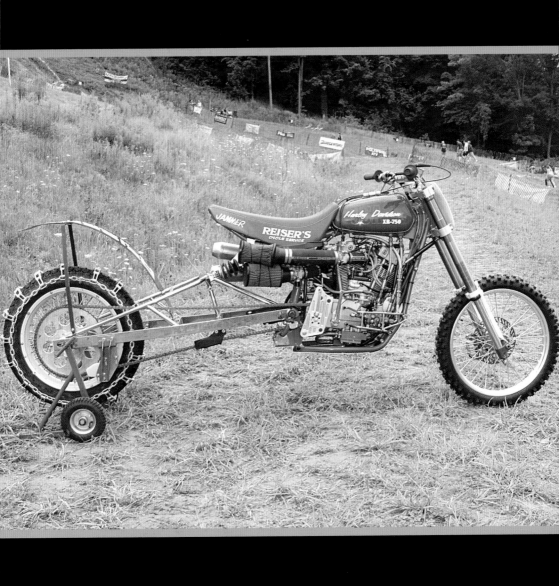

Nitro Power

Hillclimbing bikes have powerful engines. They need a lot of power to climb hills quickly. Engines come from Honda, Harley-Davidson, and other companies. The engines are **modified** to produce more **horsepower**.

These engines do not use gasoline. Instead, they use nitromethane, or "nitro." Nitro is a racing **fuel**. It explodes very easily. Engines that use it produce a lot of power. Some hillclimbing engines make almost 300 horsepower. They have more power than many car engines!

A hillclimbing bike has a small fuel tank. This small tank cuts down on weight. It carries just enough fuel for a single run.

This engine runs on nitro, not gasoline. Some racing cars use nitro, too. It is a powerful fuel.

Hillclimbing Skills

It takes skill to compete in hillclimbing. Riders must control fast, powerful bikes. They must react quickly to **obstacles** in their paths. Riders think only about getting up the hill. They know a hillclimb is won or lost in seconds.

During a run, the rear wheel digs into the ground. When it does, the front wheel lifts into the air. So, riders must be careful. They need good traction, but they do not want to flip over. They must have good balance.

The best riders always stay on their bikes. They hit jumps and fly a long distance. They may even go sideways, but they still make it to the top!

During a hillclimb, bikes can fly high in the air. Riders need a lot of skill to keep from falling.

Staying Safe

Safety is important at hillclimbs. Riders climb the hills at high speeds. Sometimes, they lose control and crash. Riders wear helmets to protect the head and face. They wear pads and tough clothing. They wear boots and gloves, too.

Riders also use a **tether**. One end is attached to a rider's wrist. The other end is attached to a switch on the engine. If a rider falls, the tether pulls the switch. It stops the engine, so the bike does not keep going.

Before a run, an official waves a green flag. It means the hill is "green," or clear for a run. Officials keep fire equipment ready, in case any nitro catches fire.

If riders make one wrong move, they may fall!
Riders need special gear to keep them safe.

Pro Hillclimbers

Each year, pros fight it out for the AMA championship. It can be hard to **predict** who will be champ. Top riders include David Watson, Walter "Tiger" Strank, and Chad Disbennett. Another top pro is James "Jammer" Large. They have all been champs.

Top pros compete in western hillclimbs, too. They include Rusty Beer and Travis Whitlock. These riders have won on some tough western hills.

In many kinds of motorcycle racing, top pros earn a lot of money, but hillclimbing is different. In this sport, pros usually do not earn much money. Most pros have other careers besides hillclimbing. They compete because they love the sport.

Walter "Tiger" Strank blasts out of the starting box. Pros such as Strank love to compete.

Let's Climb!

Ready to climb? At the top of the hill, an official waves a green flag. You take your place in the starting box. Before you start, you rev the engine to warm it up. You focus on where you will climb. Then, you take off. The nitro-burning engine makes a huge noise. You rocket up the hill!

You hit a jump and fly through the air. When you come down, you almost fall, but you twist the **throttle** and hang on. You follow in the **ruts** left by other riders. The hill gets much steeper. Your bike roars as you fly over the top. Will you have the fastest time?

A rider takes on a hill. In hillclimbing, there is just one goal — getting to the top!

GLOSSARY

amateurs (AM-uh-churz): in sports, people who compete for fun and not to earn money.

custom (KUS-tum): specially made in a certain way.

fuel (FYULE): something that burns to provide energy.

horsepower (HORS-pow-ur): the amount of power an engine makes, based on how much work one horse can do.

modified (MOD-if-eyed): changed in some way.

obstacles (OB-stuh-kuhlz): things that get in the way of going somewhere or doing something.

predict (pruh-DIKT): guess what will happen in the future.

pros (PROZE): short for professionals. In sports, pros are people who are very good at a sport and earn money competing in it.

ruts (RUTZ) : deep grooves in the ground made by wheels.

tether (TETH-ur): in hillclimbing, a rope that attaches a rider to a switch on the bike's engine. If a rider falls during a hillclimb, the tether pulls on the switch to turn off the engine.

throttle (THRAH-tuhl): the part of a motorcycle that controls how much fuel goes to the engine. Riders work the throttle by twisting a bike's handlebar grip.

traction (TRAK-shun): the grip that something has on a surface when it is moving.

FURTHER INFORMATION

Books

Hillclimbing. Motorcycles (series). Ed Youngblood (Capstone Press)

Motorcycles. Race Car Legends (series). Jeff Savage (Chelsea House)

Videos

White Knuckle Extreme: Higher Ground (Image Entertainment)

Widowmaker 2003 (Big Rock Film and Video)

Web Sites

www.bikehillclimb.com
The Bushkill Valley Motorcycle Club hosts an AMA pro hillclimb.
Click on "pictures" to see video clips of hillclimbing action.

www.kingofthehill.org
This site has information about different kinds of hillclimbing.
It has many pictures, too.

www.muskegonmotorcycleclub.com/hbike.htm
The Muskegon Motorcycle Club also hosts an AMA pro hillclimb.
This page from their web site shows the different parts of a
hillclimbing bike.

www.pro-hillclimbers.org
At this site, you can learn about western hillclimbing.
There are many photos.

www.reisercycle.com/about6.html
Visit this site to see a hillclimbing bike built by Tom Reiser. He has
built many bikes, including ones ridden by James "Jammer" Large.

INDEX